LET'S-READ-AND-FIND-OUT SCIENCE®

STAGE 1

A Safe Home for MANATEES

by Priscilla Belz Jenkins • illustrated by Martin Classen

HarperCollins*Publishers*

The Let's-Read-and-Find-Out Science book series was originated by Dr. Franklyn M. Branley, Astronomer Emeritus and former Chairman of the American Museum–Hayden Planetarium, and was formerly co-edited by him and Dr. Roma Gans, Professor Emeritus of Childhood Education, Teachers College, Columbia University. Text and illustrations for each of the books in the series are checked for accuracy by an expert in the relevant field. For more information about Let's-Read-and-Find-Out Science books, write to HarperCollins Children's Books, 10 East 53rd Street, New York, NY 10022.

HarperCollins®, ■®, and Let's Read-and-Find-Out Science® are trademarks of HarperCollins Publishers Inc.

Library of Congress Cataloging-in-Publication Data
Jenkins, Priscilla Belz.
   A safe home for manatees / by Priscilla Belz Jenkins ; illustrated by Martin Classen.
     p.   cm. — (Let's-read-and-find-out science. Stage 1)
   Summary: Describes the disappearing habitat of the Florida manatee as an introduction to the idea that each animal needs a specific place to live.
   ISBN 0-06-027149-3. — ISBN 0-06-027150-7 (lib. bdg.) — ISBN 0-06-445164-X (pbk.)
   1. Trichechus manatus—Habitat—Florida—Juvenile literature. 2. Manatees—Habitat—Juvenile literature.
[1. Manatees—Habitat. 2. Habitat (Ecology)] I. Classen, Martin, ill. II. Title. III. Series.
QL737.S63J45 1997   96-3136
599.5'5—dc20   CIP
                                                AC

Typography by Elynn Cohen 1 2 3 4 5 6 7 8 9 10 ❖ First Edition

To all who are helping to save the manatees.
P.B.J.

For my father, William Classen, whose guidance helped launch my career in art,
and my son, Martin Jr., who modeled for the last illustration.
M.C.

With special thanks to Dr. John E. Reynolds III for his expert advice.

In the quiet stillness of the warm Florida lagoon, a baby manatee swims close to his mother. She chirps to him, and he chirps back.

When she stops to munch the juicy water hyacinth, he nudges under her flipper and drinks her rich milk. Sometimes they nuzzle each other's whiskery muzzles as if they are kissing. When she goes to the surface for air, he follows. Just three months old, he is quickly learning all about his habitat.

A habitat is the place where something lives. Your home is your habitat. There you have the food, water, air, space, and shelter you need to live. Imagine what it might be like if one of these things was missing.

Since the calf's birth, the pondlike lagoon has been the manatees' habitat. Here they have found everything they need to survive. But the lagoon is changing quickly.

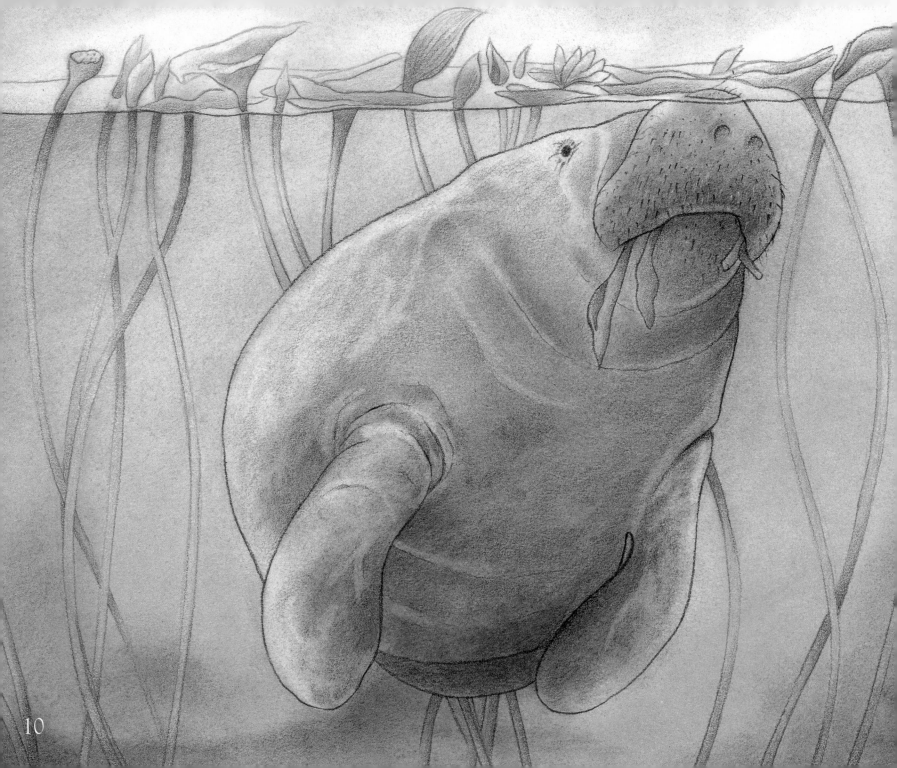

Manatees, like their distant relative the elephant, eat only plants. To satisfy their huge appetites, they spend most of their time munching over 100 pounds of water plants each day. The baby manatee's 1,200-pound, 10-foot-long mother is hungry. She cannot find enough food.

11

People are filling in the lagoon with dirt to create more land. Now the water is muddy, and light cannot reach the plants. Without light the plants cannot grow.

The calf's mother must leave to search for food.

13

From the freshwater lagoon the pair moves into the salty waters of the bay, where they cannot stay. Manatees need freshwater to drink. But it is getting harder to find, because humans have changed many of their old freshwater habitats.

The calf's mother travels the same routes her mother taught her. Now she is showing her baby the way. But people are constantly making changes to the manatee's ancient migratory routes. They dredge and fill with dirt. They build dams and canals and even change the courses of rivers! Many manatees become confused and lost.

From the bay the mother manatee finds her way to a river and freshwater. She searches for food. But where she once grazed, there are people, and boats, and danger.

Varooooom! The boats speed overhead. The mother manatee quickly drops lower. She knows what the knife-sharp propellers can do. The ugly scars on her back tell of times she could not get out of their way fast enough. Many people slow down when they see the *Caution* signs. But more and more boats keep coming.

The two manatees continue on. It is growing colder. They must find warm waters soon. They cannot survive for long below 68°F. They head north through the river's canals and locks. The tall, heavy doors to the locks open and close, letting water in or out to help boats move up and down the river. Upstream people are dredging and filling. The river is thick and mud-puddle brown.

The mother chirps to her baby. But he does not answer.
She squeals for him. Still no answer. Somehow they have
gotten separated in the muddy water. And two gigantic
doors are closing!

His mother calls again in loud squeals. Finally, a small squeal comes back to her from the other side of the doors. She moves toward the sound. The doors have not closed completely, but she cannot fit through the opening. She squeals as loudly as she can. Her baby returns her frightened calls.

Mysteriously, the doors open wider, and she quickly paddles through. Mother and calf greet each other in joyful squeaks and chirps. As they move on together, the doors thump shut.

People who operate the locks watch closely for manatees. They help them get through the massive doors safely.

On the manatees go. Finally they reach a natural warm
spring. This is a sanctuary, a protected place for manatees.
Several hundred manatees have already gathered here. But
some are leaving. So many curious divers frighten them.
Without the warm shelter of the spring these manatees
may not survive the winter.

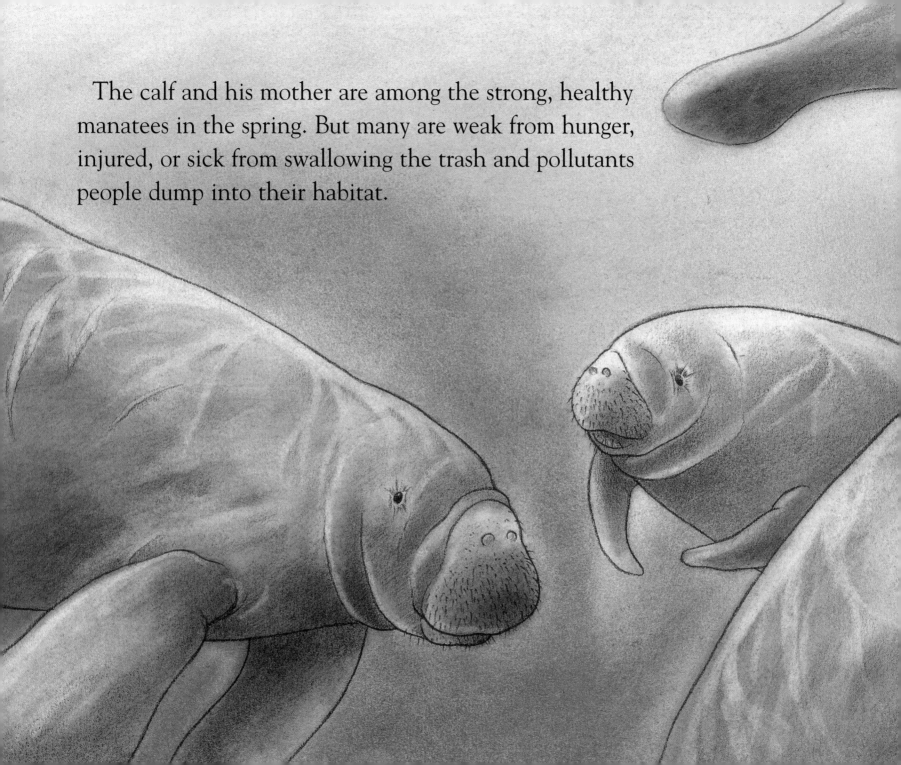

The calf and his mother are among the strong, healthy manatees in the spring. But many are weak from hunger, injured, or sick from swallowing the trash and pollutants people dump into their habitat.

For the next two years the calf will stay with his mother. With luck the winters will be mild. If we help to protect him and his habitat, one spring he will leave his mother. He will go his own way quietly munching, gently reminding us that manatees need a safe home.

Manatees, also called sea cows, are marine mammals like whales or dolphins. They feed their young milk and breathe air, as all mammals do. There are three kinds of manatees: the West Indian, which includes the Florida manatee; the West African; and the Amazonian.

Shy and very gentle herbivores, they are completely harmless. Except for mother and calf, they like to be alone. But sometimes they eat, rest, play, or explore with other manatees.

For almost fifty million years they have roamed earth's tropical lagoons, rivers, bays, and estuaries. Explorers and other seafarers, including Christopher Colombus, mistook manatees for mermaids, the beautiful half-woman, half-fish creatures of ancient myth. Once there were many thousands of manatees. But now they are in danger of becoming extinct. Today scientists believe there are fewer than 3,000 Florida manatees. Of all the dangers to manatees, the most serious is their disappearing habitat.

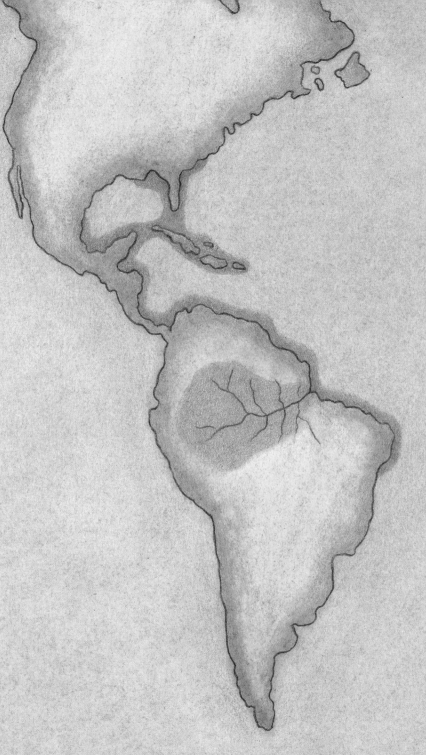

WEST INDIAN MANATEE   WEST AFRICAN MANATEE   AMAZONIAN MANATEE

YOU CAN HELP SAVE THE MANATEES.

You or your class can join the Save the Manatee® Club and adopt your own manatee. You will receive a quarterly newsletter, your manatee's name, picture, and history, and an official adoption certificate. Most importantly, you will be helping to save the manatees. You can call toll free, 1-800-432-JOIN, or write:

Save the Manatee® Club
500 N. Maitland Avenue
Maitland, FL 32751